God's Spirit Within Me

by

Carole Frankel & Sandy Wardman

Published by Tau publishing

God's Spirit Within Me

Published by Tau publishing

Phoenix, Arizona 85006

Tau-publishing.com

ISBN: 978-0-9815190-0-5

Book Layout and Design: Arlene Besore

Edited by: Carole Armstrong and Elaine Thiel

Printed in the United States of America

2008—First Edition

10 9 8 7 6 5 4 3 2 1

For re-orders and additional inspirational books, CD's, Cards and Calendars
visit our website at Tau-publishing.com

Come Holy Spirit
Come into my life.

How can I live in JOY?

I sing a happy song.
I sing praises to God.
I sing everyday.

*The Holy Spirit puts a happy song
in my heart.*

I smile often.
I laugh with my family
  and friends.
I'm glad to be with others.

The Holy Spirit helps me laugh.

I bounce up and down.
I skip when I'm happy.
I'm playful and friendly.

*The Holy Spirit fills my heart
with happiness.*

I clap and dance.
I shout and cheer.
I raise my hands in joy.

*The Holy Spirit dances
within me.*

How can I live in

Gentleness?

I learn about nature.
I smell the flowers.
I look for beautiful things that
    God made.

*The Holy Spirit shows
me beauty.*

I take care of animals.
I show my friends how.
I care for life.

*The Holy Spirit helps me
help others.*

I make a friend.
I listen and care.
I share with others.

*The Holy Spirit guides me
in all that I do.*

I read books with Grandma.
I find quiet time.
I thank God for family.

*The Holy Spirit brings
me peace.*

How can I live in Faithfulness?

I help my Papa shop.
I obey my elders.
I love my family.

The Holy Spirit blesses me.

I watch over my brothers,
    sisters, and friends.
I teach them about God.
I do my best all the time.

The Holy Spirit leads me.

I keep trying even when things are
    hard to do.
I ask God for help.
I praise God if I'm sad.

The Holy Spirit makes me strong.

I talk to God every day.
I thank God for all of my blessings.
I tell God how much I love Him.

The Holy Spirit helps me pray.

How can I live in
Goodness?

I follow the rules.
I choose the right way.
I am careful.

The Holy Spirit watches over me.

I pick up my toys.
I do my chores.
I complete each job.

The Holy Spirit reminds me.

I help smaller children.
I do not argue.
I tell the truth.

The Holy Spirit is with me.

I prepare for visitors.
I make special foods.
I welcome my guests.

The Holy Spirit helps me.

How can I live in

Patience?

I take my time with chores.
I help my brother with his.
I stay calm.

The Holy Spirit guides me.

I stand quietly.
I breathe deeply.
I feel God all around me.

The Holy Spirit calms me.

I let others help me.
I wait my turn.
I smile my thanks.

The Holy Spirit blesses me.

I sit with my friends.
I read good books.
I think about God.

The Holy Spirit inspires me.

How can I live in

Self Control?

I mind my parents.
I respect my grandparents.
I listen to my teachers.

The Holy Spirit leads me.

I forgive those who hurt me.
I pick myself up.
I control my anger.

The Holy Spirit protects me.

I learn from others.
I wait to speak.
I pray for God's help.

The Holy Spirit blesses me.

I speak good about others.
I walk away from bad talk.
I think happy thoughts.

The Holy Spirit guides me.

How can I live in

Kindness?

I sort clothes.
I fill the bags.
I give to the poor.

The Holy Spirit is with me.

I comfort those who are sad.
I sit with them.
I tell them God loves them.

The Holy Spirit shows me love.

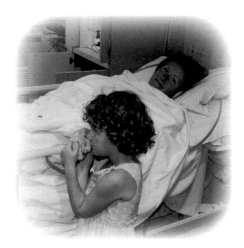

I pray for those in the hospital.
I pray for their families.
I ask God to heal them.

The Holy Spirit answers me.

I visit my neighbors.
I bring food.
I share my time.

The Holy Spirit blesses my gifts.

How can I live in Peace?

I am nice to my brother.
I am gentle with my sister.
I talk with my friends.

The Holy Spirit guides me.

I read the Bible.
I think of God.
I share my thoughts about God.

The Holy Spirit inspires me.

I pray in church.
I close my eyes.
I am silent.

The Holy Spirit is quiet in me.

I sit outside.
I hear the wind.
I feel the warm sun.

*The Holy Spirit breathes
peace into me.*

How can I live in

Love?

I play with my friend.
I play fair.
I bring my friend to my house.

The Holy Spirit loves me.

I care for all God's creatures.
I feed them.
I bring them water.

The Holy Spirit is with me.

I write a letter to my grandfather.
I call my grandmother on the phone.
I tell my parents I love them.

The Holy Spirit shows me love.

I tend a garden.
I water the plants.
I pull the weeds.

The Holy Spirit brings me
new life.

Activities for God's Spirit Within Me

Dear Parents and Teachers,

The following are activities to reinforce the concepts of living with God's spirit within. They are designed to inspire activities at home or in the classroom to develop this awareness.

To help your child or your class to participate, you can write words and lists for preschool children. You can expand and add to any of these ideas. Pray to God and ask Him to show you how to help the children. He wants every child to know Him. He will help you.

Sincerely,
Carole Frankel and Sandy Wardman

Activities for Living in Joy

Independent Activities

1. Make up a song and sing it to your family. Sing your new song to God.
2. Listen to music you like to hear. Make up a praise dance. Dance your new dance for God.
3. Make a list of five people who bring you joy. Write down what they do to bring you joy.
4. Make a list of things you can do to bring people joy.
5. Write or draw a picture of ways you feel joy.

Activities with Family and Friends

1. List on a chart what brings you and others joy.
2. Cut pictures from magazines. Make a collage of things, people or places that bring you joy.
3. Stand in a circle and play "Ring Around the Rosy" and other musical games.
4. Sing songs together. Clap the rhythm.

Classroom Activities

1. List on a chart what brings you and others joy.
2. Think of an activity from that list that you can do to bring joy to a classmate or your teacher.
3. Plan and paint a class mural showing those things that bring you joy.
4. Play musical games with your classmates.
5. Sing songs together. Skip with friends.
6. Make funny faces. Laugh with your friends.

Activities for Living in Gentleness

Independent Activities

1. Plant flower seeds in a garden or pot. Take care of the plants and watch them grow. Make a chart of their growth.
2. Find a special place to read. Pick a time to read. Sit quietly in your special spot and read a book every day.
3. Hug a pet or a stuffed animal.

Activities with Family and Friends

1. Ask a family member or a friend to read to you.
2. Walk outside. Draw a picture of each type of plant you see. Make a book of plants.
3. Visit a zoo with your family. Draw pictures of animals and make a book.

Classroom Activities

1. Play "Pass the Egg" (Ping pong balls can be used in place of eggs)
   - Divide up into pairs with one person as Person A and the other as Person B.
   - Stand in two lines—the A's in the starting line and the B's in a line opposite the A's. Make the space in between the two lines as large as possible.
   - The A's begin with A holding an egg in a teaspoon. The A person must carry the egg with one hand across the empty space to their B partner without dropping the egg.
   - Pass the teaspoon to the B partner without dropping the egg. Both partners can only use one hand.
   - Race to the starting line. The team that arrives at the starting line first wins.
2. At the playground, play nicely with others.
3. Let others go first in line.
4. Sit with someone new and share a story about yourself.

Activities for Living in Faithfulness

Independent Activities
1. Make a list of chores you do to help your family.
2. Every time you do a chore, put a star on the list.
3. With each star, thank God that you could help.
4. Make a list of things that are hard for you to do. Pray to God to help you.
5. Read your Bible every day.

Activities with Family and Friends
1. Give everyone in your family a hug and tell them you love them.
2. Play a game with your brothers and sisters. Tell them about God.
3. Ask your family to pray with you. Set a special time every day to pray with your family.

Classroom Activities
1. Play a circle game of trust.
   - Stand in a circle.
   - Turn to the right so that you are facing the back of the person next to you.
   - Move toward the center of the circle until you are touching the people next to you.
   - On the count of three, bend your body to sit down on the knees of the person behind you.
   - Do you have faith that the person behind you will not fall?
2. Make a chart of things you do every day at school. Check each off as you complete them. Examples include:
   - Pick up paper that is on the floor in your classroom.
   - Put supplies back where they belong.

Activities for Living in Goodness

Independent Activities
1. Make a list of rules that your parents ask you to follow.
2. Put a star on the list every time you follow a rule.
3. Thank God that you could follow the rule.

Activities with Family and Friends
1. Invite friends over to your house.
2. Prepare something special for them to eat.
3. Go to the park with your friends. Count how many rules you can follow.
4. Help smaller children in your family and in the park.

Classroom Activities
1. Make a list of rules you must follow in your classroom.
2. Make another list of rules you must follow in your town or community.
3. Discuss why it is important to follow the rules.
4. Pick a rule from your classroom. On the count of three, everyone breaks it. For example, break the rule of no shouting by having everyone shout. Be sure and have a cue to stop the shouting.
5. Make a list of consequences. What happens when people do not follow the rule?

Activities for Living in Patience

Independent Activities
1. Find a quiet place to go when you are upset, tired or nervous.
2. Go to your quiet place and take ten deep breaths. Say "I love you God" every time you inhale.
3. Say these words; "I am calm. I am patient." Repeat five times. Write them on a paper.
4. Help a family member today with one of their chores.

Activities with Family and Friends
1. Invite a friend to play a game with you. Wait your turn.
2. Sit with your friends and take turns reading a good book.
3. Go to the library during story time. Sit quietly and listen to the story.

Classroom Activities
1. Make a list of all the things you know about God.
2. Paint a mural that shows what the class listed.
3. Pick one of the items from that list that helps you to have patience.
4. Make a picture that shows how that item makes you feel.

Activities for Living in Self-Control

Independent Activities
1. Decorate a box and tuck it under your bed.
   - Every time someone makes you angry, draw a picture of what happened. Put the picture in the box.
   - Before you climb into bed, take out your box and say a prayer for each person in the box.
2. Don't listen to children who make fun of others. Walk away. Change the conversation. Talk about how God wants us to live.

Activities with Family and Friends
1. Sit with your family or friends and discuss challenges faced that day. Make a list of how each challenge was handled.
2. If you said something bad or hurt someone today, tell them you are sorry. You can do this by telling them in person, calling them on the phone, drawing a picture or writing a note.
3. Ask first, before you touch something that is not yours.

Classroom Activities
1. Choose a word everyone uses (pencil, paper, or chair). Make a game where the word you chose is not allowed to be used. The winner will be the last person who doesn't use that word.
2. Play musical chairs.
   - Everyone in class places their chairs in a circle and sits.
   - The teacher plays music and whenever the music plays, the students must get up from their chairs and walk in a circle in front of the chairs.
   - Each time the music plays, take away one chair.
   - Stop the music. Everyone must sit down. The child who doesn't have a chair is out of the game.
   - Continue until there is only one chair left. The child who sits in it wins.

Activities for Living in Kindness

Independent Activities
1. Sort through your clothes and your toys and put what you don't use or need anymore into a box. Ask your parents to donate the box to the needy.
2. If your parents are tired or sad, make them a picture and tell them you love them.
3. Pray for people you know who are ill or alone. Ask God to help them.

Activities with Family and Friends
1. Ask your parents to take you to visit someone you know who is alone. They could be a neighbor, someone in the hospital or in a nursing home.
2. Make a picture or bake cookies for the person you will visit.
3. Sit with your family or friends and each tell about an act of kindness they did that day.

Classroom Activities
1. Make a list of acts of kindness.
2. Discuss and decide what act of kindness the class can do as a class project. This could include such things as collecting food, toys, clothing, etc for the needy; helping prepare food for the homeless; reading stories to the younger pre-school class.
3. Plan and prepare for an act of kindness and do it.
4. Help your teacher put away toys or pick up papers. Offer to help before or after class.

Activities for Living in Peace

Independent Activities
1. Go outside and look for God in nature. Sit quietly and listen to the sounds around you.
2. Pray and talk to God. Tell Him about your life.
3. Write a prayer of thanks to God.
4. Draw a picture of your favorite place. Close your eyes and picture yourself there.
5. Hang a wind chime outside. When it rings, think about God.

Activities with Family and Friends
1. Ask your family to take you to a place where people pray.
2. Ask your parents if you can say grace before the family meal. Thank God for your food and family.
3. Say something nice to each person in your family and to each one of your friends.
4. Go to a bookstore or library and find relaxing music. Sit with family or friends and listen to the music.

Classroom Activities
1. Read Philippians 4:8-9. Make a list of the things that are true, right, honest, pure, lovely, admirable, or excellent.
2. Find pictures that show these words and make a collage.
3. Read this list every day and feel the peace from the Holy Spirit.

Activities for Living in Love

Independent Activities
1. Make a special prayer book and put your prayers in the book.
2. Each morning, choose a prayer from your prayer book and talk to God about it.
3. Take special care of the animals in your house and your neighborhood. Play with them. Ask if you can feed them a treat.

Activities with Family and Friends
1. Call your grandparents and tell them you love them.
2. Draw a picture or write a letter to a friend or family member who lives far away and mail it to them.
3. Tell everyone in your family that you love them. Hold their hand and give them a hug.
4. Make a new friend today. Invite them to play with you.

Classroom Activities
1. List the nine fruits of the spirit (joy, gentleness, faithfulness, goodness, patience, self-control, kindness, peace, love).
2. Make a mural that shows these words. Put these words under the heading: Strive For
3. Every day read these words aloud and feel the love of the Holy Spirit enter the classroom.
4. Start a food or herb garden. Help take care of the garden. Pick the ripe vegetables or herbs and share them with others.